ROYAL COURT

Royal Court Theatre presents

THE WORLD'S BIGGEST DIAMOND
by **Gregory Motton**

First performance at The Royal Court Jerwood Theatre Upstairs
Sloane Square, London on 28 October 2005.

T0348079

THE WORLD'S BIGGEST DIAMOND

by **Gregory Motton**

Cast in order of appearance
Mrs Thomas **Jane Asher**
Mr Smith **Michael Feast**

Director **Simon Usher**
Designer **Anthony Lamble**
Lighting Designer **Simon Bennison**
Sound Designer **Emma Laxton**
Production Manager **Sue Bird**
Stage Managers **Nafeesah Butt, Francesca Finney**
Costume Supervisors **Iona Kenrick, Jackie Orton**
Company Voice Work **Patsy Rodenburg**

The Royal Court would like to thank the following for their help with this production:
Bush Theatre, English Touring Theatre, Greco Brothers Ltd www.grecobrothers.co.uk,
Keep Able www.keepable.co.uk, Mr Tea www.mrtea.co.uk.

THE COMPANY

Gregory Motton (writer)
For the Royal Court: Ambulance, Downfall, The Terrible Voice of Satan.
Other theatre includes: Chicken (Riverside Studios); Looking at You (Revived) Again (Leicester Haymarket); A Message for the Broken Hearted (Liverpool Playhouse); Cat and Mouse (Sheep), In Praise of Progress (Théâtre de L'Odeon, Paris); A Little Satire (Gate); A Monologue (Musée Daupinois, Grenoble); God's Island (Théâtre de la Tempête, Paris); Gengis Amongst the Pygmies (La Comédie Française, Paris).
Translations include: Miss Julie, The Father, Creditors, The Comrades, The Burned Site, The Ghost Sonata, The Storm, The Pelican, The Black Glove, The Great Highway, The Dance of Death I and II, Swanwhite, Easter, The Name, Nightsongs, Someone is Going to Come, Woyzech.
Radio includes: The Jug, Lazy Brien.

Jane Asher
For the Royal Court: The Shallow End, Look Back in Anger (& Criterion), The Philanthropist (& Mayfair/Broadway), Treats (& Mayfair).
Other theatre includes: Romeo & Juliet, Measure for Measure, Cleo, Great Expectations, The Happiest Days of Your Life, Sixty Thousand Nights (Bristol Old Vic/USA tour); Old Flames (Bristol Old Vic); Strawberry Fields, To Those Born Later, The School for Scandal, House/Garden (RNT); Whose Life Is It Anyway? (Savoy); Peter Pan (Shaftesbury); Before the Party (Queen's); Blithe Spirit, Henceforward (Vaudeville); Making It Better (Hampstead/Criterion); Things We Do for Love (Guildford/Gielgud); What the Butler Saw (Bath/tour); Festen (Almeida/Lyric).
Television includes: New Tricks, Miss Marple, Crossroads, The Choir, Murder Most Horrid, Wish Me Luck, The Mistress, Bright Smiler, East Lynne, A Voyage Around My Father, Love Is Old, Love Is New, Brideshead Revisited, The Mill on the Floss.
Film includes: Tirant lo Blanc, Closing Numbers, Paris by Night, Dream Child, Success is the Best Revenge, Runners, Henry VIII and his Six Wives, Deep End, Alfie, Greengage Summer.

Simon Bennison (lighting designer)
For the Royal Court: Black Milk.
Other theatre includes: The Price (Tricycle/West End); Home, Serjeant Musgrave's Dance, Comedians, The Contractor, Troilus and Cressida (Oxford Stage Company); Normal, Howie the Rookie, Yard (Bush); Holes in the Skin (Minerva); Scenes From an Execution, A Lie of the Mind (Dundee Repertory Theatre).
Dance includes: Ghosts; Before the Tempest after the Storm, Asyla, Broken Fiction, Sophie, Stateless, Between Shadows, Unstrung Tension, Three Words Unspoken, Traces (Cathy Marston); Out of Denmark (Johann Kobberg/QEH); The Lesson, Renard (Royal Ballet); Pointless (George Piper Dances/Roundhouse); Sea of Troubles (Adam Cooper/English National Ballet); Afsked (Kim Brandstrup); Palimpsest (Shobana Jeyasingh); Last Night at The Empire, Tick (Tom Sapsford).
Opera includes: Carmen (English Touring Opera).
Simon trained in lighting and design at RADA and the Yale School of Drama, and in architecture at the University of North London.

Michael Feast
For the Royal Court: Prairie de Chien, The Shawl, Ourselves Alone.
Other theatre includes: American Buffalo, No Man's Land, The Tempest, The Forest, Dispatches, Watch It Come Down, The Mentalists (RNT); The Alchemist, Carousel, Skin Of Our Teeth, Present Laughter (Royal Exchange Manchester); The Possessed (Almeida); Measure for Measure, Murder in the Cathedral, Faust I & II (RSC Stratford/London); After Darwin, Clever Soldiers (Hampstead); The Servant, Oliver Twist (Lyric Hammersmith); The Beggar's Opera (Wilton's Music Hall); The Cherry Orchard (English Touring Theatre); The Accused (Theatre Royal Haymarket); The Seagull, Nathan The Wise, Master & Margarita, Faustus (Chichester Festival).
Television includes: Trial & Retribution, The Virgin Queen, Jericho, Murphy's Law (Series III), Absolute Power, Peter Ackroyd's London, Boudica, Ultimate Force, State of Play, Young Blades, The Stephen Lawrence Case, Midsomer Murders, Get Well Soon, Touching Evil (Series I, II and III), Casualty, Kavanagh, Bugs, A Touch of Frost, No Final Truth, Inspector Alleyn, Underbelly, Resnick, Clarissa, Boon, South by South East, Paradise Club, Shadow of the Noose, Studio, Nightwatch, Blind Justice.
Film includes: Long Time Dead, Sleepy Hollow, Prometheus, The Tribe, Miss Marple, A Caribbean Mystery, The Fool, McVicar, The Draughtsman's Contract, Bother Sun Sister Moon, Private Read.

Anthony Lamble (designer)

For the Royal Court: Incomplete and Random Acts of Kindness, Mother Teresa is Dead, Herons.

Other theatre includes: Sing Yer Heart Out For The Lads, A Midsummer Night's Dream, As You Like It, Translations (RNT); Measure For Measure, Richard III, The Roman Actor, King Baby (RSC); Home, Singer, Comedians, The Contractor, Troilus and Cressida (Oxford Stage Company); Macbeth (Dundee Rep); A Christmas Carol, In Celebration, Aristocrats, Spell of Cold Weather, The Sea, School of Night, Insignificance, The King of Prussia, Retreat from Moscow (Chichester Festival); Lettice and Lovage, Exquisite Sister, Burning Everest (West Yorkshire Playhouse); Card Boys, All Of You Mine, Mortal Ash, Pond Life, Not Fade Away, Evil Doers, Looking At You (Revived) Again (Bush/Leicester Haymarket); Someone Who'll Watch Over Me, The Roman Actor, The Price (West End); Longitude (Greenwich); Cleansed, Release the Beat, Owner Occupier (Arcola).

Anthony Lamble has also designed shows for Leicester Haymarket, Sheffield Crucible, Almeida Music Festival, English Touring Theatre, The Gate, Riverside Studios, the Lyric Hammersmith, Croydon Warehouse, Paines Plough, and Shared Experience. He is also a tutor for the Motley Theatre Design Course.

Dance and opera includes: Facing Viv (English National Ballet); L'Orfeo (Purcell Quartet in Tokyo); Palace in the Sky (ENO); Baylis (Hackney Empire); Broken Fiction (Royal Opera House).

Film includes: A Secret Audience.

Emma Laxton (sound designer)

For the Royal Court: Incomplete and Random Acts of Kindness, My Name is Rachel Corrie, The Weather, Bear Hug, Bone, Food Chain, Terrorism.

Other theatre includes: Parade (Southside, Edinburgh Fringe), The Gods Are Not to Blame (Arcola Theatre), Maid's Tragedy (White Bear), The Suppliants (BAC), Break Away (Finborough), The Unthinkable (Sheffield Crucible); My Dad is a Birdman (Young Vic), Party Time/One for the Road (BAC); As You Like It, Romeo and Juliet (Regent's Park Open Air Theatre).

Head of Sound at Regent's Park Open Air Theatre in 2001 and 2002.

Emma is Sound Deputy at the Royal Court.

Simon Usher (director)

For the Royal Court: Herons, Mother Teresa is Dead, Black Milk.

Other theatre includes: Timon of Athens, The Broken Heart, The Bells, Pale Performer, Looking at You (Revived) Again, Murders in the Rue Morgue, The Naked, Pericles, French Without Tears, Lettice and Lovage, The War in Heaven, The Lover's Melancholy, Trios, The Winter's Tale (Leicester Haymarket); King Baby, Tamar's Revenge (RSC); Sing Yer Heart Out for the Lads (RNT); The Evil Doers, Pond Life, Not Fade Away, The Mortal Ash, All Of You Mine, Wishbones, Card Boys (Bush); Burning Everest, Exquisite Sister (West Yorkshire Playhouse); Twins (Birmingham Rep); Mr Puntila and his Man Matti, Holes in the Skin (Chichester); Les Liaisons Dangereuses, Waiting For Godot, Heartbreak House, The Browning Version, Hamlet, Whole Lotta Shakin' (Coventry Belgrade); Great Balls of Fire (Cambridge Theatre, West End); No Man's Land (English Touring Theatre); The Wolves (Paines Plough); Can't Stand Up For Falling Down (Watford).

THE WORLD'S BIGGEST DIAMOND

First published in 2005 by Oberon Books Ltd
521 Caledonian Road, London N7 9RH
Tel: 020 7607 3637 / Fax: 020 7607 3629
e-mail: info@oberonbooks.com
www.oberonbooks.com

Copyright © Gregory Motton 2005

Gregory Motton is hereby identified as author of this play in
accordance with section 77 of the Copyright, Designs and Patents
Act 1988. The author has asserted his moral rights.

All rights whatsoever in this play are strictly reserved and
application for performance etc. should be made before
commencement of rehearsal to Gregory Motton, care of Oberon
Books at the above address. No performance may be given unless
a licence has been obtained, and no alterations may be made in
the title or the text of the play without the author's prior written
consent.

This book is sold subject to the condition that it shall not by way
of trade or otherwise be circulated without the publisher's consent
in any form of binding or cover or circulated electronically other
than that in which it is published and without a similar condition
including this condition being imposed on any subsequent
purchaser.

A catalogue record for this book is available from the British
Library.

ISBN: 9781840026252

Cover image: Gregory Motton / Jeff Knowles @ Research Studios

Characters

Mr Smith

He is seventy-three years old,
a bit frail, unwell.

Mrs Thomas

She is sixty, a lawyer.
On the surface she is brisk and alive.

I

In his bedroom in an old house by the coast. A large room with a fireplace (downstage) with an armchair beside it. Also a small tea table with two antique chairs, near the door (upstage). He is sitting in the armchair by the fire. She comes in wearing her coat.

Mrs Thomas   Is it the room upstairs above this one?

Mr Smith   Yes, that's right

Mrs Thomas   Wait, okay? I'll be back in a minute.

She goes out onto the stairs. Calls out to her husband upstairs: 'Gareth! It's that one there. No. That one. That's it.'

Mr Smith sits and listens to her voice.

——

Some while later. They are sitting at a small table in the room, near the door. She has taken her coat off and it is now hanging behind her chair.

Pause.

Mrs Thomas   I could stay and look after you.

Mr Smith   Nurse me to my death do you mean?

Mrs Thomas   Yes, if you like.

Mr Smith   No thank you.

Pause.

Mrs Thomas   I always expected to do it. (*Pause.*) And anyway...

Mr Smith   What?

Mrs Thomas (*Pause.*) Well, it's the only one of my hopes concerning you that can possibly be realised now, isn't it.

Mr Smith Unless you would like to try for children?

Mrs Thomas (*Silence.*)

Mr Smith What is it now?

Mrs Thomas I don't have a sense of humour.

Mr Smith I know you haven't but I thought we'd have a bit of a laugh anyway.

Mrs Thomas I didn't know we were expected to laugh about that.

Pause.

I'd gladly swap places with you. It's a matter of complete indifference to me.

Mr Smith What is?

Mrs Thomas Living or dying. Or I'll come with you if you like.

Mr Smith You've been saying that ever since you were nineteen. I don't like it any more now than I did then.

Mrs Thomas You should have liked it. I meant it then and I mean it now – I'd quite like us to die together.

Mr Smith Don't you mind your husband hearing that?

Mrs Thomas He knows. Obviously. Look, I think I had better go and help him with the bags and so on.

Mr Smith Oh. Alright.

Mrs Thomas And then we said we'd go for a walk.

Mr Smith Did we?

Mrs Thomas Gareth and I.

Mr Smith Oh. I see. Yes. Alright then.

Mrs Thomas Were you about to say something?

Mr Smith No.

Mrs Thomas Oh.

Mr Smith Of course if I'd taken you up on it, even in those days...

Mrs Thomas I would have been surpised. (*Laughs.*)

Mr Smith You would have declined, is more to the point.

Mrs Thomas And that would have let you nicely off the hook wouldn't it?

Mr Smith Do you remember your chosen means of death?

Mrs Thomas No.

Mr Smith You wished that the badly-made shelves over your bed would fall on our heads while we slept. Your law books would have killed us.

Mrs Thomas Yes I remember now.

Mr Smith And which of us then would have guessed that you would have turned those books into a comfortable life and a thriving Paris practice, with a successful husband to go with it?

Mrs Thomas Right, I think that's enough of that don't you?

Mr Smith Enough of what?

Mrs Thomas I never wanted any of those things. I would have made do with an unsuccessful husband and no career at all, just the two children with you that I wanted.

Mr Smith Why is it that when you make bitter remarks you are the victim, but if I try to make a bitter remark you are still the victim.

Mrs Thomas That's because I am the victim.

Mr Smith And you're going to keep that up right to the end are you?

Mrs Thomas Yes.

Mr Smith (*Pause. He looks at her.*) You've got that charnel-house look in your eyes, I can see.

Mrs Thomas (*She looks at him in surprise.*)

Mr Smith What is it now?

Mrs Thomas Nothing. It's just, well it's so long since you said that. So long...it reminds me...

Mr Smith What?

Mrs Thomas Of everything.

Mr Smith Everything. And does it remind you how much I loved you?

Mrs Thomas (*A little miserably.*) I don't know.

Mr Smith Oh.

———

II

Next day. On the sea front. She accompanies him, he is in a motorised chair.

Mrs Thomas You don't say anything. Is the light too strong?

Mr Smith It hurts.

Mrs Thomas Let me put up the shade.

Mr Smith No. Blast the shade. It's useless.

Mrs Thomas Put on your sunglasses then.

Mr Smith I don't want to. It looks ridiculous.

Mrs Thomas All right. Close your eyes. Rest them. Sleep.

Mr Smith I'm not a baby. I don't sleep in the afternoon. I never have.

Mrs Thomas No alright.

Mr Smith You're the one who sleeps in the afternoon.

Mrs Thomas Me?

Mr Smith You always used to.

Mrs Thomas When I was young I did. I slept all the time.

Mr Smith Yes you did. All day and all night. You were quite nice when you were asleep.

Mrs Thomas I think you preferred me that way.

Mr Smith Yes.

Mrs Thomas I liked to sleep beside you. It's thirty years since I slept in the afternoon.

Mr Smith Well I don't either.

Mrs Thomas All right. Those days are gone.

Mr Smith Is there anything else you are presuming about me on account of my age or state of health?

Mrs Thomas No.

Mr Smith You may have presumed that I can't still get it up. Well, I can reassure you that I can.

Mrs Thomas (*Laughs.*) I didn't say you couldn't.

Mr Smith I can prove it if you like.

Mrs Thomas Are you asking to have sex with me?

Mr Smith What's so odd about that?

Mrs Thomas Nothing is odd about it. Nothing.

Mr Smith Well then. Don't behave as if there is.

Pause.

Mrs Thomas You certainly aren't in the habit of asking me.

Mr Smith No.

Pause.

Well I haven't seen you for about ten years.

Mrs Thomas Of course you have.

Mr Smith Hardly. Only when your husband is there too.

Mrs Thomas He's here now.

Mr Smith Yes but now I don't care.

Mrs Thomas You never cared.

Mr Smith Yes I did. I kept right away. I kept right out of it.

Mrs Thomas Oh yes, you kept right away. You didn't want to prevent me from falling in love, I suppose.

Mr Smith That's right.

Mrs Thomas You wanted me to be able to settle down.

Mr Smith Exactly

Mrs Thomas This time.

Mr Smith What?

Mrs Thomas This last time. With Gareth. Unlike the first two times.

Mr Smith ...the first two times?

Mrs Thomas Yes!

Mr Smith The first two times.

Mrs Thomas Stop repeating it. The first two men, the first two times.

Mr Smith Oh I see. Yes. Well what about them?

Mrs Thomas You didn't keep away then did you.

Mr Smith Yes I did!

Mrs Thomas Don't be ridiculous. You didn't.

Mr Smith Do you mean...

Mrs Thomas ?

Mr Smith Do you mean...that I...about when I...cried on the phone?

Mrs Thomas No I don't mean that.

Mr Smith Oh.

Pause.

Good.

Pause.

Good, because that was only the first year. The first year or two. I wasn't very well...

Mrs Thomas Yes I know.

Mr Smith That was understandable. Well, wasn't it?

Mrs Thomas Yes.

Mr Smith You do think so?

Mrs Thomas Yes. I've never said it wasn't have I?

Mr Smith No.

Pause.

You were bloody horrible to me.

Pause.

Mrs Thomas I know. Let's not go over that, not now. I've said I'm sorry. You know why I did it. I was barely alive.

Mr Smith Alright let's skip that.

Mrs Thomas Yes, let's skip it.

Pause.

Mr Smith But the first two, I kept right away as I remember it.

Mrs Thomas Not quite.

Mr Smith Well, we stayed in contact if that's what you mean?

Mrs Thomas You tried to make sure that they meant nothing to me

Mr Smith Did I? How?

Mrs Thomas You asked me.

Mr Smith I can't have asked you!

Mrs Thomas You did.

Mr Smith Oh. Well. And did they?

Mrs Thomas What?

Mr Smith Mean nothing.

Mrs Thomas Yes.

Mr Smith Was that my fault?

Mrs Thomas Who else's fault was it.

Mr Smith It was hard for me to keep track of them. They got the chop pretty quickly.

Mrs Thomas Whose fault was that?

Mr Smith Not mine. You always were pretty touchy. I remember you nearly finished with me once because I raised my voice to you on a tube train.

Mrs Thomas I didn't like brawling in public.

Mr Smith Yes, you were very dignified for a twenty-one year old.

Mrs Thomas Would you like to stick to the point?

Mr Smith Yes.

Mrs Thomas The point is, you were always there. You never let me go. I clung on to you and you let me. Because you wanted me to.

Mr Smith You didn't cling on, you got married. Twice. Three times!

Mrs Thomas Yes, exactly. Three times.

Mr Smith Once or twice could be a mistake, but three times…

Mrs Thomas Are you saying it was a mistake for me to get married?

Mr Smith No, I was joking.

Mrs Thomas This isn't a joke. This is my life. God!

Mr Smith (*Pause.*) We don't have to talk about your marriages you know.

Mrs Thomas I know. I don't mind though, if you need to.

Mr Smith Well, I don't mind either. If you need to.

Mrs Thomas I don't need to. I thought you did.

Mr Smith I don't. No.

Pause.

Look at those blasted seagulls!

Mrs Thomas What's wrong with them?

Mr Smith Nothing. They can't help it. (*Pause.*) It's always like this – you've established this crazy history of what happened. My version will never be heard. Like all histories from the loser's point of view, it remains unwritten.

Mrs Thomas I was the loser, not you. And being allowed to write the history is my consolation prize. Why don't you forget it, it's too late now.

Mr Smith As usual you don't ask me to say what my version is.

Mrs Thomas No, I don't.

Mr Smith 'No, I don't,' you say. As if it's the most natural thing in the world.

Mrs Thomas Shall we go inside. It's getting too windy to hear anything anyway. My ears hurt.

Mr Smith Alright.

Mrs Thomas My nose is running. Do you have a handkerchief?

Mr Smith No. I never have a handkerchief.

Mrs Thomas Well my nose is running…

Mr Smith Well wipe it on my sleeve then.

Mrs Thomas I will not wipe it on your sleeve.

Mr Smith Why not? Alright wipe it on your own sleeve.

Mrs Thomas Give me your arm then.

She wipes her nose on his sleeve.

They go in.

———

III

In his room. She has just finished helping him to settle into his chair by the fire.

Mrs Thomas There.

Mr Smith Thanks. Are you going to stay in here with me for a while?

Mrs Thomas Yes, not for too long though.

Mr Smith Well, do you want to or not?

Mrs Thomas Yes.

Mr Smith It doesn't sound like it.

Mrs Thomas I do. I'm here aren't I?

Mr Smith I don't know, it's hard to tell with you.

Mrs Thomas Well, I promise you I am here.

Mr Smith (*Pause, looks about him.*) Well, that's funny.

Mrs Thomas You're not being very nice.

Mr Smith Do you have to go back upstairs to Gareth?

Mrs Thomas Well, eventually.

Pause.

Mr Smith I am afraid, you know that don't you.

Silence.

Afraid of dying.

Mrs Thomas Yes, well…

Pause.

Mr Smith You aren't very sympathetic.

Mrs Thomas You know why that is.

Mr Smith Could you remind me?

Mrs Thomas How typical that you forget that I have offered to die with you.

Mr Smith I haven't forgotten it. I refuse to acknowledge it.

Mrs Thomas I don't see why.

Mr Smith I naturally want to keep you from harm, I suppose.

Mrs Thomas I'd rather you wouldn't, it's not actually very romantic.

Mr Smith Of course it is.

Mrs Thomas No. I know you love me but if you were passionate, you would think differently.

Mr Smith I am passionate – I love you…as I love myself.

Mrs Thomas Yes well. That's not.

Mr Smith Not…?

Mrs Thomas Not enough. It's not the same as passion.

Mr Smith Well Christ!

Mrs Thomas Passion is desire. Wanting to have me with you wherever you go, even in your grave.

Mr Smith And should I be able to disregard your welfare?

Mrs Thomas Nothing unusual there.

Mr Smith I see.

Mrs Thomas An all-consuming love...would snuff out our lives.

Mr Smith You know why you think like this don't you? It's not entirely to do with love.

Mrs Thomas I'd rather you didn't go on.

Mr Smith Why not?

Mrs Thomas I don't want to hear that you find me unsuitable to be with you after we are dead.

Mr Smith Annihilation is what you want. It's because you were depressed as a child. You wanted your father to save you from your wicked stepmother by killing you and himself. Then you found me to take his place.

Mrs Thomas Well it's terribly far-fetched. You've gone way over the top; I suppose it must be your age, it sounds much more ridiculous now than when you were younger.

Mr Smith I still had all my faculties then. Nowadays I say something that sounds fine to me, and then I hear later it was ridiculous.

Mrs Thomas Life isn't that elaborate. It's all simple. I loved you and wanted you. You loved me and only cared for me. It doesn't matter what the reason is. Everything has a reason.

Mr Smith If you won't see the reason for something you might not be able to see *what* it is.

Mrs Thomas I should go to bed now. I don't really want to have this kind of long painful conversation any more. The time for them is gone.

Mr Smith The time for them has just arrived!

Mrs Thomas Stop shouting or I'll leave at once.

Mr Smith (*Pause.*) You never want us to say anything about the reason for us not being able to stay together.

Mrs Thomas No I don't.

Mr Smith You've gone your whole life without understanding.

Mrs Thomas (*She stands and looks at her watch.*) I understand all too well; I don't want to know.

Mr Smith You say that from a great height as if it doesn't concern you.

Mrs Thomas It doesn't any more.

Mr Smith You pretend what happened is a moral unpleasantness, quite beneath you.

Mrs Thomas I don't see why it has anything to do with me.

Mr Smith That's only because you won't accept any responsibility – that's what distorts everything.

Mrs Thomas I am going to bed now. Gareth is waiting up for me. Goodnight.

Mr Smith ...responsibility for me being married when we met.

Mrs Thomas It wasn't my fault.

Mr Smith Wasn't it? (*He takes a deep breath, he has never said this before.*) You saw my wife and children even before you saw me.

Mrs Thomas Oh I see. So this is what it finally boils down to. I wish I had known this was the level we were on, I could have saved myself all the trouble.

Mr Smith Face the truth, just this once! You saw them.

Mrs Thomas It wasn't my responsibility.

Mr Smith Are you sure?

Mrs Thomas Yes.

Mr Smith Also, I told you from the start that I would never leave them.

Mrs Thomas At the beginning, yes. Somewhat over-emphatically I remember.

Mr Smith Yes, you said so at the time.

Mrs Thomas Anyway, I thought it was what you said to every girl you went to bed with, just in case, to cover yourself.

Mr Smith Charming.

Mrs Thomas I didn't know it applied to me. I didn't know it applied to me after we had fallen in love.

Mr Smith We fell in love on the first day, that's why I said it.

Mrs Thomas I didn't know it applied to me, considering what she had done and after we had been in love for two years.

Mr Smith I said it because I loved you, not in case I would love you.

Mrs Thomas I didn't know it still applied to me after we had been in love for six years, and I still don't understand and I still don't want to hear what the reason is for you leaving me, and if you ever tell me the reason I think I shall drop down dead on the spot. I've dreaded it all my life.

Mr Smith There's nothing harmful to you in it, and yet you have harmed yourself all your life because you won't hear it.

Mrs Thomas Don't speak any more.

Mr Smith Here it comes whether you like it or not and this is what you have dreaded hearing for forty years: You wanted unconditional love from me but you wanted me to abandon someone else for doing wrong.

Mrs Thomas I think this is really rather disgusting.

Mr Smith You wanted faith from me but you wanted me to be faithless. You wanted to be unique in my eyes but you wanted me to treat someone else as interchangeable.

Mrs Thomas Have you finished?

Mr Smith Have I finished? What do you mean? Yes, I've finished.

Mrs Thomas Then you are an even bigger criminal than I have always thought you to be.

Mr Smith And what is my crime?

Mrs Thomas To try to love me in the first place.

Mr Smith Then it is a crime of passion.

Mrs Thomas How could it be when what you have just said shows you were incapable of passion!

She leaves the room, slamming the door behind her.

Mr Smith (*Not calling after her, but as if she is still there.*) Upside down. She hasn't learnt anything at all. You haven't bloody changed since you were a girl. Smug look on your face.

———

IV

That night. 4 am. Indoors. He is sitting on a chair by a window, a blanket around his feet. A small lamp or candle on a small antique table. Outside the window, a rainstorm.

There is a tiny knocking on the bedroom door.

Mr Smith Come in.

She comes in. She's wearing a nightdress, bare feet, and an outdoors overcoat over it.

Mrs Thomas Hello? Am I disturbing you?

As she comes in she stubs her toe on a chair leg which is very painful. She cries out in a muffled tone.

Ow. Ow. Ow.

Mr Smith What have you done?

Mrs Thomas I hit my toe. On your chair.

Mr Smith Oh dear. (*Pause.*) Is it alright?

Mrs Thomas No. I think it's broken.

Mr Smith Really? Oh dear.

Mrs Thomas Oh!

Mr Smith Let me see.

Mrs Thomas No it's alright. Leave it. Oh!

She moans a little, she waits for the pain to subside.

A hiatus.

Mr Smith (*In sympathy.*) Alright now?

Mrs Thomas Yes.

Mr Smith Good.

Pause.

How come you're up?

Mrs Thomas I can't sleep.

Mr Smith Haven't you slept at all?

Mrs Thomas No.

Mr Smith You look as if you've been fast asleep.

Mrs Thomas I might have dropped off.

Mr Smith I know all about your insomnia. You sleep right through it.

Mrs Thomas (*She knows this. Heaves a tired sigh.*) I'm on my way to the loo.

Mr Smith There's a perfectly good chamber-pot under your bed. Pink. Minton.

Mrs Thomas You should have told me then.

Mr Smith Do you mean you haven't looked under the bed?

Mrs Thomas No I haven't.

Mr Smith I see. Aren't you interested any more?

Mrs Thomas I don't dare look under the bed. I don't even dare look at pictures on the walls.

Pause.

Don't forget how painful it is for me to come here. To stay in your house. I think I should have stayed in a hotel.

Mr Smith You tried to. They were full up.

Mrs Thomas So, you're still awake?

Mr Smith Of course I am. Have you ever known me to go to sleep before five o'clock?

Mrs Thomas I don't know, you might have changed your habits.

Mr Smith Because I'm ill do you mean?

Mrs Thomas No, I just mean anyway.

Mr Smith Of course I haven't.

Mrs Thomas I wouldn't know would I?

Mr Smith You always try to pretend we don't know each other any more.

Mrs Thomas No, you always pretend nothing has happened, as if time stood still thirty years ago. It's cowardly.

Mr Smith I don't see how it's cowardly.

Mrs Thomas As if by pretending no harm was done, and nothing was lost, you make it so.

Mr Smith We still have what we still have, I'm not going to wish that away.

Mrs Thomas It seems easy for you to pretend. Maybe I was no great loss to you.

Mr Smith I'm not pretending, *you* are.

Mrs Thomas I'm not going to trick myself into forgetting we lost each other just by playing sentimental little games about how well we know each other.

Pause.

Mr Smith Misery sounds more convincing, doesn't it, to you.

Mrs Thomas That's because I don't forget what it all really amounts to.

Pause.

Mr Smith Well, I've got some tea on the fire there; you can put some coal on, save me having to do it.

Mrs Thomas You've got a very nice little arrangement.

Mr Smith Arrangement?

Mrs Thomas I just mean your kettle on the fire.

Mr Smith You sound like a stranger.

Mrs Thomas You've managed to shut out the present entirely. (*Laughs.*)

Mr Smith Oh yes, that's right.

Mrs Thomas Yes.

Mr Smith I like to hide from reality.

Mrs Thomas I didn't mean that.

Mr Smith I'm not ashamed of it. It's just like the eighteenth century in here, isn't it?

Mrs Thomas Yes, it's very clever.

Mr Smith Good. You ought to like it.

Mrs Thomas You know I do, so stop pretending I don't.

Mr Smith I prefer the lies of the past to the lies of the present.

Mrs Thomas Yes I know you do.

Mr Smith The older I get the more I find myself on the side of everything that has been swept away. It could have been a beautiful world, but it isn't…

Pause.

Mrs Thomas I think it's perverse and sentimental to keep faith with something that was defeated.

Mr Smith Do you really? I'm shocked to hear you say that.

Mrs Thomas Don't you understand? It's useless to me. I'm a woman, I'm a human being. I'm flesh and blood. I live and feel on the level of flesh and blood. I have spent my life, because of you, in defeat after defeat of my flesh and blood. I don't understand anything else, nothing else touches me, this can't touch me. You can't touch me. I wish you could but I am beyond your reach. It makes me very sad to hear you try, and to know how useless it is, how far off we are from one another.

Pause. He sighs.

Mr Smith Which one of us is it?

Mrs Thomas What?

Mr Smith Both of us seem to think we are the keeper of the true flame of our love and that the other is trying to blow it out.

Long pause.

Mrs Thomas Blowing it out and keeping it alight, both look the same.

Pause.

But you ought to know that it's me that bears the true flame.

Mr Smith You say that, but I'm not sure I believe it.

Mrs Thomas However could it be otherwise?

Mr Smith Because you try to destroy it out of resentment.

Mrs Thomas Maybe.

Mr Smith You think proving something about it is better than being able to enjoy our love…as best we can.

Mrs Thomas I don't enjoy it.

Mr Smith You may even think destroying it puts you in the right.

Mrs Thomas You don't call these polite fantasies *Love*, do you?

Mr Smith …because you think your destructive gesture is the one sign of real love.

Mrs Thomas In the circumstances, yes.

Mr Smith Because you believe in gestures. I don't.

Mrs Thomas It's not a gesture, it's true love.

Mr Smith To kill it?

Mrs Thomas Perhaps.

Mr Smith This terrible frame of mind you have. It's pure but I'm not sure it is ultimately good.

Mrs Thomas No I know. It's not. And I'm not good. I may even be the opposite. But at least I know what love is.

Mr Smith We are talking ourselves into blackness.

Mrs Thomas Yes, I'd better go back to bed.

Mr Smith I'd rather you'd stay for a cup of tea.

Mrs Thomas Yes I know you would, to try to un-say all that has been said, but I don't want to.

Mr Smith As you wish. Life is quite short though. Too short perhaps for purification by fire every day.

Mrs Thomas (*Relents on account of his illness.*) I know. I'm sorry.

Mr Smith Oh I didn't mean just for me – I mean it's too short for all of us.

Mrs Thomas No it is not short. It's long. Far too long.

She exits in tears.

———

V

The next day, noon. Bright sunshine in the room. She comes in with a tray of food, a fried breakfast. He wakes up from being asleep in his chair. He finds the light too bright for his eyes.

Mrs Thomas I brought you breakfast.

Mr Smith Did you now? That's nice. What is it?

Mrs Thomas Here. I may have burnt some of it.

Mr Smith Hmm. (*Laughs.*)

Mrs Thomas Is that alright?

Mr Smith It's perfect yes. (*He sets himself to begin eating.*) Do you remember what you used to bring me for breakfast?

Mrs Thomas No, I'm afraid I don't.

Mr Smith Blueberries, milk and oats.

Mrs Thomas I don't remember.

Mr Smith Don't you?

Mrs Thomas Well, now you say it, perhaps…

Mr Smith How sad. I thought you'd remember that. (*He shies from the light.*) Could you…

Mrs Thomas Is it too bright? Shall I draw the curtains?

Mr Smith Just a bit. That's it. I've been kicked in the head by a donkey.

Mrs Thomas When?

Mr Smith In my sleep.

Mrs Thomas Oh. (*Pause.*) Is it good enough? (*The food.*)

Mr Smith Yes it is.

Mrs Thomas I thought you meant me.

Mr Smith Who?

Mrs Thomas The donkey.

Mr Smith Oh. Yes, I might have done. But I didn't. Yes I might well have done. Eeyore! (*The noise.*) Eeyore. (*The name.*)

Mrs Thomas We're going home tomorrow.

Mr Smith What?

Mrs Thomas Yes, at about six. Is that alright?

Mr Smith (*Taken aback.*) No it's not all right.

Mrs Thomas Why not?

Mr Smith Why do you think?

Mrs Thomas I don't know. I can't stay forever.

Pause.

Eat your breakfast.

He eats his breakfast.

Stops. It's hard to chew, his mouth is dry.

What's the matter? Don't you like it?

Mr Smith I can't chew. My mouth is dry.

Mrs Thomas Have some tea. (*Lifts up his cup for him.*)

Mr Smith Why can't you?

Mrs Thomas What?

Mr Smith Stay forever.

Mrs Thomas (*Ignoring him.*) Is six o'clock alright?

Mr Smith ...after all forever isn't all that long.

Mrs Thomas (*Ignoring him.*) Six o'clock.

Mr Smith Well, I'm hoping to last a little longer than that...

Mrs Thomas You've no right.

Mr Smith What?

Mrs Thomas To ask me to stay.

Mr Smith Why not...?

Mrs Thomas You've no respect for me at all.

Mr Smith ...why not, I mean you yourself offered.

Mrs Thomas Did I?

Mr Smith Yes you offered to stay and nurse me until I died, now you're leaving tomorrow. I don't get it.

Mrs Thomas Well, you said no.

Mr Smith You don't even remember do you?

Mrs Thomas Of course I do. You said no.

Mr Smith How could you forget asking me that.

Mrs Thomas It doesn't matter if I remember or forget –

Mr Smith – you're in the right either way.

Mrs Thomas – no, because I would stay and nurse you until you die if you asked me.

Mr Smith Well I don't intend to die before six o'clock tomorrow just to save you from being a hypocrite.

Mrs Thomas The thing is, you don't ask me, and you never will.

Mr Smith Will you please stay and nurse me until I die. There.

Mrs Thomas You don't mean it. You will never ask me properly. Which is why I'm leaving tomorrow. I'll come back, don't worry. Of course.

Mr Smith At the end. When the final whistle blows.

Mrs Thomas (*No reply. She laughs involuntarily at his metaphor.*)

Mr Smith Well I think it's very odd. I ask you to stay, and you refuse on the grounds that I haven't asked you.

Mrs Thomas That's right. Anyway, we've booked the car ferry.

Pause. He tries to eat some more breakfast.

Alright, so, if you'd like to go for a walk with me later, let me know, but don't leave it to the last minute.

Mr Smith Will you sit down.

Mrs Thomas I'm packing.

Mr Smith Bollocks. You haven't even unpacked.

Mrs Thomas How would you know?

Mr Smith You think that just because I can't get upstairs to your room that I haven't been through your bags and your clothes and looked at the stains on your sheets and held your toothbrush. You underestimate me, my girl.

Mrs Thomas There are no stains on my sheets. You won't even have to wash them.

Mr Smith I won't be washing them. I'll pay Mrs Whatsit to bring them down and put them on my bed.

Short pause.

Which side have you been sleeping on by the way?

Mrs Thomas Left.

Mr Smith Alright. Would you put a mark on the top so I don't mix them up?

Mrs Thomas Yes.

Mr Smith So.

Mrs Thomas I'll be ready for a walk by half past two.

Mr Smith A roll do you mean?

Mrs Thomas A roll yes. I'll roll you along the front.

Mr Smith But tell me, why are you in such a rush?

Mrs Thomas You see. No respect. I've got a husband for a start. Do you think he likes being here?

Mr Smith Why not? It's very pleasant. We all get along really well, I thought.

Mrs Thomas Oh yes.

Mr Smith I'm really nice to him and he's really nice to me. I like him very much.

Mrs Thomas He likes you.

Mr Smith There you are then.

Mrs Thomas He also likes me.

Mr Smith Does he? Then we've even more in common.

Mrs Thomas And he finds it very painful to be here.

Mr Smith Is this necessary?

Mrs Thomas Why wouldn't it be? You asked.

Mr Smith I didn't ask that.

Mrs Thomas Ask what?

Mr Smith About your marriage. I don't want to know that
he finds it painful to be here.

Mrs Thomas Don't you? Don't you want to know that
someone loves me?

Mr Smith Of course I want you to be loved.

Mrs Thomas Do you want me to have a dry empty life,
just to reassure you, for your peace of mind, so you
know you have no rivals in my heart. Is that it? Is that
how much you love me?

Mr Smith I've...been through all that thirty years ago. I'm
used to it. I just don't want to hear about it.

Mrs Thomas (*With sympathy.*) I know.

Pause.

(*Without sympathy.*) Or were you hoping that by now it
will have worn off? And I would have settled down to
a loveless old age, and that my life will have once again
returned to being a pure shrine to My Perfect Love For
You? Did you hope that?

Mr Smith Well I'm not going to say no, but I also hoped
the opposite. Yes, each night around the time you get out
of your shower and lay down in your bed, I hoped it,
then I ran away and thought about something else.

Mrs Thomas Or did something else yourself.

Mr Smith (*Sighs.*)

Mrs Thomas (*Angry from the image created in her mind by her last comment.*) So I don't think he should have to endure more of it than is necessary.

Mr Smith I see.

Mrs Thomas I'll go now, and I'll see you at half past two.

Mr Smith Yes.

———

VI

Same day, two-thirty. On the sea front.

Mr Smith There are various reasons why you should stay. Should I go through them before you leave?

Mrs Thomas It's a bit late really.

Mr Smith It's a bit late. I see. Well I will anyway.

Mrs Thomas Alright.

Mr Smith One is: I think you want to stay.

Mrs Thomas No I don't.

Mr Smith Yes. I think you do. In fact how could you not? I certainly hope that you do.

Mrs Thomas Alright.

Mr Smith You bloody well ought to.

Mrs Thomas Ought to?

Mr Smith Yes. If you love me as you claim to.

Mrs Thomas That doesn't follow. In theory maybe, but in practice, no.

Mr Smith How can you leave a man to go through his last months on his own, when he is the man you love?

Mrs Thomas Do you have any other reasons?

Mr Smith Yes. (*Pause.*) I'm afraid of being seperated from you, in case it's forever.

Mrs Thomas Well... (*Pause.*) That's all very well but...

Mr Smith I'm terrified...of that.

Mrs Thomas I don't even think it's sincere.

Mr Smith Oh you don't do you?

Mrs Thomas How can I, after thirty-five years?

Mr Smith I can't remember any of it. All I can remember is the last two nights. You were upstairs. I was in my bedroom... I was in another place, with no shape, and no end. It was like the universe, my room became like the universe and I was floating. Last night, long after you'd gone back to your room, I called out to you but you were asleep.

Mrs Thomas I wasn't. I was awake.

Mr Smith You mean you heard me?

Mrs Thomas Yes.

Mr Smith Really?

Mrs Thomas Yes.

Mr Smith Why the hell didn't you come?

Mrs Thomas I was at your door in seconds.

Mr Smith Oh were you? What, outside the door?

Mrs Thomas Yes, I listened at your door.

Mr Smith I was terrified. I wish you had come in!

Mrs Thomas I was afraid that me being there wouldn't help, and you'd realise you didn't need me, in this life or any other.

Mr Smith How long do you intend to postpone finding out?

Mrs Thomas I don't ever want to know.

Mr Smith But…I'm…crying out for you in my last… agonies.

Mrs Thomas No you aren't.

Mr Smith Well almost. I will be soon. In a few months. And you won't be here.

Mrs Thomas I was never here.

Mr Smith You are now.

Mrs Thomas It's just someone. You want someone. It's bad luck for you that it happens to be me.

Mr Smith Good luck surely.

Mrs Thomas No, it's bad luck. Because I can't stay. I can't stay because you've left it too late.

Mr Smith It's not someone. I've got Mrs Whatsit. If I want just someone. She's very nice. She's no fool you know. We have a good time together. She's very witty.

Mrs Thomas Get Mrs Whatsit to stay then.

Mr Smith She has pains in her arms.

Mrs Thomas I'm not surprised.

Mr Smith She can't go out most days. She has to drag herself here.

Mrs Thomas I bet.

Mr Smith Are you jealous of Mrs Whatsit?

Mrs Thomas No.

Mr Smith You're the most jealous woman I have ever met. Or have ever heard of. Or even read about.

Pause.

What do you do if Gareth is unfaithful?

Mrs Thomas He isn't.

Mr Smith Wasn't he? Ever?

Mrs Thomas Of course not. I would have left him immediately. I didn't marry him so that he could do that to me. If I'd wanted that I could have stayed with you.

Mr Smith I was never unfaithful to you!

Mrs Thomas You were permanently unfaithful to me, because you stayed with your wife! Don't you see! You can't undo it, and that's why you must be alone now.

Mr Smith I can't believe you mean it.

Mrs Thomas Yes.

Mr Smith You mean you will row with me right up until I die? And then into eternity? That's a very extravagant way of making a point.

Mrs Thomas (*Silence.*)

Mr Smith My bloody ears are freezing.

Mrs Thomas Put your hat on.

Mr Smith It is on.

Mrs Thomas Oh yes. Well, then we can go back.

Mr Smith Alright. And then you go to bed, and then you get up, and then it's goodbye forever.

Mrs Thomas Yes. (*Pause.*) Except that I'll be coming back later.

Mr Smith So you say.

Mrs Thomas Yes.

Mr Smith What if you're too busy? What if there's an important trial? What if a top murderer needs your help to avoid punishment? What if an illegal immigrant needs you to get his teeth mended at the taxpayers' expense?

Mrs Thomas Then I shan't be able to come.

Mr Smith (*His attention transfers to his fingers.*) I can't believe how wrinkled the skin of my hands has become. It's amazing.

Mrs Thomas They're not all that wrinkled.

Mr Smith It's horrible. Like a lizard.

Mrs Thomas It's worse for me. My breasts are hanging.

Mr Smith There's nothing wrong with your breasts.

Mrs Thomas You don't see them.

Mr Smith And Gareth does I suppose.

Mrs Thomas Of course he does.

Mr Smith Do you mind sparing me the details. I prefer not to know.

Mrs Thomas You prefer to pretend that my husband doesn't see my breasts??

Mr Smith Yes.

Mrs Thomas You're still about seven years old.

Mr Smith Sweet isn't it? Now, shall we get some ice cream?

Mrs Thomas In this wind?

Mr Smith Are you afraid it will blow into your face?
Would you feel foolish if it went into your eye?

Mrs Thomas What?

Mr Smith I remember you getting ice cream into your
eye. You thought it was undignified.

Mrs Thomas What are you talking about?

*He looks at her for a long time. She stands completely still.
Then he comes away from his memories.*

Mr Smith My memory has improved with age. I know
more about you now than ever before. I remember it all.

Mrs Thomas Yes I see.

Mr Smith Whereas I had forgotten some of it.

Mrs Thomas Thank you.

Mr Smith Not much but some. But now I remember it
all. I resent you much more now I remember how very
unfairly you treated me, whereas at the time I forgot it
very quickly didn't I?

Mrs Thomas Yes I liked you for it. Don't spoil that.

Mr Smith Oh yes, you like your crimes to be forgotten.
And you know why? Because you think you have a right
to do wrong don't you? Admit it.

Mrs Thomas Yes alright. And where is the ice cream?

Mr Smith I just made a very important point about you.
Are you going to ignore it?

Mrs Thomas I heard it.

Mr Smith Yes I know you heard it.

Mrs Thomas Where is the ice cream, I don't see any?

Mr Smith It's right there. You'll have to run across the road and get it.

Mrs Thomas Give me the money then.

Mr Smith I haven't got any.

Mrs Thomas Oh, I'm paying am I?

Mr Smith Well, yes. You are.

Mrs Thomas What flavour?

Mr Smith Fucking Banana, what do you think?

Mrs Thomas Vanilla.

Mr Smith Yes.

Pause.

He watches her. Adoringly.

Some gulls come very close, so close that he bats them away with his arm, but his eyes remain upon her.

She returns.

The gulls depart.

She gives him an ice cream.

It's thirty years since we split up.

Mrs Thomas Yes.

Mr Smith It's like sailing out to sea, then looking back expecting to see to where you have come from but the land is no longer even in sight.

Mrs Thomas Yes. It's been a long voyage.

Mr Smith (*Pause.*) In reality though, I always kept pretty close to the coast.

Mrs Thomas That would explain why you never got anywhere then, my darling.

Mr Smith Yes it would explain that.

Mrs Thomas We woke up with a room full of smoke last night.

Mr Smith Did you really?

Mrs Thomas The smoke from your fire seemed to have leaked into the top room. Maybe your chimneys are broken.

Mr Smith Yes I think they are. Apparently it's the feather wall or something between my fire and the upstairs one. It has corroded away. Hundreds of years of salt water in the air.

Mrs Thomas Well maybe you should get it seen to.

Mr Smith Yes.

Mrs Thomas The smoke could have killed us.

Mr Smith Oh. Yes. Oh dear. I'm sorry about that.

Mrs Thomas No it's alright, but someone else... You have all kinds of people staying in that room.

Mr Smith Oh all kinds.

Mrs Thomas People you wouldn't like to kill.

Mr Smith Yes.

Mrs Thomas You should take care.

Mr Smith I will.

Mrs Thomas Can't you get them swept or something?

Mr Smith It's not as simple as that. It's a very complicated and difficult process. And it costs a fortune.

Pause.

Mrs Thomas Yes. I see.

Mr Smith They have to be mended from inside, by dropping a rubber forma inside it and pumping it up then shooting it full of liquid concrete, to line the walls of the chimney with it.

Mrs Thomas I see. You weren't trying to kill us were you?

Mr Smith Which then solidifies inside and it strengthens the chimney. (*Pause.*) No, of course I wasn't.

Pause.

My skin is almost transparent.

Mrs Thomas Not really.

Mr Smith Thank God I gave up smoking when I did, otherwise I'd be in really serious trouble. He's not more intelligent than me is he?

Mrs Thomas Of course not, no one is. You're the cleverest man in the whole wide world.

Mr Smith I know I am like a child sometimes when I'm with you but that just…well it's an aspect of our relationship.

Mrs Thomas Yes, I know.

Mr Smith It's not the only aspect.

Mrs Thomas I realise that.

Mr Smith You're the child too sometimes…

Pause.

…as we well know.

Mrs Thomas Merci.

Mr Smith Yes and I'm…that's not what I am actually like, you know that.

Mrs Thomas I've known you for thirty-five years.

Mr Smith Yes of course but you might have forgotten and fallen into mistaken habits of thinking about me that are not accurate.

Mrs Thomas Don't worry, I'd never do that.

Mr Smith You've always done it.

Mrs Thomas Only through mistrust, not poor judgment.

Mr Smith Good. Yes. Okay.

She takes her shoes off to walk barefoot.

What are you doing?

Mrs Thomas Taking my shoes off.

Mr Smith What for?

Mrs Thomas Because I like to feel the sand on my feet.

Mr Smith There isn't any sand, we're on the pavement.

Mrs Thomas Well, there is a little bit.

Mr Smith I'm glad you're having a nice trip to the seaside! I'm glad you are able to enjoy it! I'm glad nothing stops you being able to take the opportunity to feel the sand on your feet!

Mrs Thomas Don't be silly. (*Pause. She keeps her sandals off.*) You seem agitated.

Mr Smith Yes, I feel a bit rushed, to say things before, well before you go off back to…your office…or your home. You know.

Mrs Thomas Yes. You'll be fine. You'll be fine for a while until I come back.

Mr Smith Oh yes. I'll be fine. Of course I wasn't trying to kill you both. Do you think I'd want to send you two to your graves together, you two together?

Mrs Thomas No, I suppose not.

Mr Smith What a horrible surprise that would be!

Mrs Thomas Who for?

Mr Smith Well…for me. Mainly. I'd be left behind, after thinking I'd go first.

Mrs Thomas (*Pause.*) I don't want to be left behind without you.

Mr Smith I don't think it bothers you that much.

Mrs Thomas How little you know. It has always seemed more or less pointless to be alive, but once you're gone… I find it almost humiliating to think of it…

Mr Smith But, my darling, you're thirteen years younger than me.

Mrs Thomas Thirteen – unlucky for some.

Mr Smith You must expect me to go first. And then you can wait around a bit and join me later.

Mrs Thomas I don't think it's funny to wait around.

Mr Smith (*New subject.*) I keep wondering what you two talk about in your room. I stare at the ceiling listening. Your voices, it goes on all night! What the bloody hell are you talking about?

Mrs Thomas Oh, nothing. Just chatting.

Mr Smith Don't say just chatting. That's the worst possible thing you could say and you know it.

Mrs Thomas You surely don't mind be me being able to chat to my husband?

Mr Smith My husband. My husband. What in the name of God are you chatting about at four in the morning?

Mrs Thomas He's working on something at the moment. He likes to talk to me about it.

Mr Smith Does he? Whatever for?

Mrs Thomas Don't let's argue.

Mr Smith I've always thought The Arts is work for homosexuals. Do you know what I mean? I mean, it's not real work is it. Don't you feel a bit sick after a day in court with people who have been murdered or run over, to have to come home and listen to a homosexual whinging about what dance steps to use, or what colour to paint the fucking set, or if the baton would look best stuck sideways up his arse?

Mrs Thomas Have you finished?

Mr Smith It's all just rubbish after all isn't it?

Mrs Thomas Yes, it's all just rubbish.

Mr Smith Art is a job for homosexuals.

Mrs Thomas I heard you the first time.

Mr Smith It's true.

Mrs Thomas You can put it in your next book then can't you?

Mr Smith I intend to. There's only one thing worse than a homosexual artist.

Mrs Thomas And what's that?

Mr Smith A bisexual one. It's because their egos are so big. One sexuality isn't enough to feed it, they need two. It's greed. They resent being restricted to just one. They want more money, more praise, more power, more cock, more cunt then anyone else.

Mrs Thomas As you know, my husband is not a homosexual or a bisexual.

Mr Smith Isn't he? No, of course. Well, I wasn't talking about him. You didn't think I was did you?

Mrs Thomas There's something a bit odd about what you're doing.

Mr Smith Odd? Yes you're right, there is. Very odd, it's very odd. You mean what? By that word? Do you mean sick or perverted or insane or dishonest or desperate or what is it you mean exactly? Because on its own 'odd' means nothing very much. I know it's your favourite accusation. But it means fuck all. Do you ever prosecute anyone for being odd? In court, do you? And how do you go about proving it?

Mrs Thomas I don't like this.

Mr Smith No, you don't do you. But that's because you've got no taste and no sense of humour. You ought to be able to enjoy it but you are too much of a prig. You guard your honour as if it were the world's biggest diamond, but I've good reason to think that it isn't.

Mrs Thomas I don't know why you want to insult me.

Mr Smith I don't. I just happen to be describing you and it comes out as an insult. I told you it all nearly fifty years ago.

Mrs Thomas Thirty-five years. I remember.

Mr Smith Pity you didn't do anything about it.

Mrs Thomas What could I have done?

Mr Smith You could have stopped being such a prig and a hypocrite.

Mrs Thomas I have stopped now.

Mr Smith (*Pause.*) Have you? That sounds ominous.

Mrs Thomas I'm completely different now, from when you knew me.

Pause.

Mr Smith Oh. (*Pause.*) What a shame. I fell in love with a hypocritical little prig and now you are fair and open-spirited, not at all what I grew to expect of a woman... perhaps you've become a homosexual too?

Mrs Thomas (*Laughs.*)

Mr Smith It must get very hard to work out where to put the baton between you.

Mrs Thomas Have you done now?

Mr Smith I wish there were some point in carrying on.

———

VII

Same day, late evening. In his room. There has been some loud knocking on the front door of the house which has remained unanswered and has finally stopped. They are finishing a cup of tea. He has a newspaper which he pretends to read from:

Mr Smith '"I'm very sick in the head," said the man. Sentencing is tomorrow.' (*He folds the newspaper and throws it away.*)

Mrs Thomas Why does Mrs Whatsit knock on your door like that?

Mr Smith She knocks because she can't see the bell. Yes it's a funny thought. She's as blind as a stone, and yet she earns her living as a cleaner. How does she do it?

Mrs Thomas Maybe all her employers are blind like you and can't see any dust she misses.

Mr Smith I'm not blind. I don't know what you mean. I've just had my eyes checked only yesterday. Nearly perfect, he said… Anyway, she doesn't dust. She merely…puts things away.

Mrs Thomas Why don't you put them away yourself?

Mr Smith I don't know where they go. Mrs Whatsit has secret places. Either that, or she's taking it all home with her. I can't find it at any rate.

Mrs Thomas You mean she's stealing it?

Mr Smith She's welcome to it, if she is.

Mrs Thomas So your cleaner is selling your personal effects already?

Mr Smith No. She has grandchildren who look after that side of things.

Mrs Thomas It sounds very well organised.

Mr Smith It is. They pick her up from here and drive her away in a car. She can't carry her bags herself you see, they're too heavy, it hurts her fragile arms.

Mrs Thomas How old is she, this Mrs Whatsit?

Mr Smith She's twenty-six.

Mrs Thomas What?

Mr Smith No, forty-six.

Mrs Thomas She's very young for a grandmother.

Mr Smith She was the town's youngest mother, she was fifteen.

Mrs Thomas What did she want at this time of night?

Mr Smith She calls in on her way back from bingo on the front. I don't usually let her in but she always knocks.

Pause. She wanders to the window, as if she is trying to imagine his life there.

Mrs Thomas Do you have any other neighbours? Do they mind you?

Mr Smith Oh yes, Chummy next door says I make a lot of noise, although quite how he thinks I do it, he won't say.

Mrs Thomas I bet you do make noises.

Mr Smith Noises, yes I expect I do. I am after all living, and I am doing it here. 'I have lived in detached properties all my life,' says Chummy, 'but now I'm trying to get used to other people's noise,' which he does mainly by telling them to be quiet.

Mrs Thomas Maybe he's lonely.

Mr Smith Yes he's lonely, although he does have a friend living with him. I believe they are living in sin.

Mrs Thomas Don't you know their names?

Mr Smith Chummy and Chummy as far as I know. Chummy informs me he is a bohemian. He had a short piece of organ music on Radio 3 in 1980. He is much admired, by Chummy, whom he treats like a skivvy. Are you pleased I'm making friends?

Mrs Thomas I'm very relieved. How often do you see them?

Mr Smith Every time I make a noise; they come round to ask me to be quiet.

Mrs Thomas Both of them?

Mr Smith No. Chummy normally sends the tart. He won't come himself for fear of seeming to be a tedious narrow-minded old cunt.

Mrs Thomas How do you make the noise?

Mr Smith With my walking stick. I bang it on the floor, before I make my announcements to Mrs Whatsit. (*He bangs his stick three times on the floor.*) They'll be round in a minute, would you like to meet them?

Mrs Thomas We don't have enough time to waste it on them.

Mr Smith It's not a waste. It's fun, it's a laugh, you'd love it.

Mrs Thomas I wouldn't. I'd hate it. They won't really come will they?

Mr Smith No, they've gone to Morocco looking for little boys to bugger.

Mrs Thomas Have they?

Mr Smith Unless they go for the bathing facilities and the vibrant ethnic folk markets.

Mrs Thomas I wish you'd stop it. You sound like Colonel Blimp.

Mr Smith (*Laughs.*) Who? I'm not that kind of man. For God's sake woman, I'm low class, you ought to remember that. This morning for example, I've been on my knees scrubbing the floors. I like it.

Mrs Thomas But you can hardly walk.

Mr Smith Well I have anyway.

Mrs Thomas Well, I'm glad you're enjoying yourself.

Mr Smith (*Ignores her attempt at banter.*) The worst of it all is...

Mrs Thomas What?

Mr Smith (*Pause.*) ...that I can't sing any more.

Silence.

I used to love singing.

Mrs Thomas You can still...can't you?

Mr Smith My voice, it's ruined, it's gone. Imagine! Not being able to sing! I might as well be dead.

Mrs Thomas At least you have sung, in the past.

Mr Smith Oh I have, have I? My whole life is wasted. I didn't sing enough! What the hell was I doing? When I was little, I sat on my bed all night, singing like a bird. I'm a natural singer, that's what I *am*.

Mrs Thomas You have sung.

Mr Smith No but it's what I am. I forgot. I forgot it, I knew...and somehow I forgot. It's awful. I can't bear to think of it.

Mrs Thomas You used to sing all the time.

Mr Smith That wasn't singing.

Mrs Thomas Wasn't it? It sounded like singing

Mr Smith Listen. Don't fuck me about. You knew you could always sing better than I could, so you know all about it.

Mrs Thomas I don't, really. I knew you could sing, that's all I know.

Mr Smith Let's not talk about it.

Pause.

Mrs Thomas What's the matter? (*Pause.*) Sweetheart. (*Pause.*) What is it? You're crying.

Mr Smith It wasn't all my fault though. It was a lousy twenty or thirty years wasn't it, for everyone? I don't think I was the only one. Thirty years without poetry and without hope. Wasted our lives.

Mrs Thomas Yes.

Mr Smith You know when it went wrong for me? It was when I lost my brother.

Mrs Thomas You didn't have a brother, you had a sister.

Mr Smith Eh?

Mrs Thomas You said brother.

Mr Smith I mean Peter. I mean my best friend, Peter, remember?

Mrs Thomas Of course I do. I mean, I know who you mean. You were twelve.

Mr Smith I was thirteen. He was sixteen. From this distance it doesn't matter if he was a brother or a friend... Actually I get him mixed up with a few other people, all the people I've loved, I call them Peter.

Mrs Thomas Except me.

Mr Smith Maybe I'll call you Peter, towards the end.

Mrs Thomas You'd better not.

Mr Smith (*Laughs.*) No, I'd better not. It has all rolled into one, but it means the same, do you understand?

Mrs Thomas I don't know.

Mr Smith All the meanings are right. It's the names are wrong. I can see clearer and feel clearer now than

ever before. And one thing I know is that this land is
condemned.

Mrs Thomas What?

Mr Smith This land… (*Corrects himself.*) No, I mean I really
loved him. Or I do now. Then he was just a friend, but
now, now I love him. He's been dead for sixty years.
Four times longer than he lived. I love him in the same
way that I love the world. And –

Mrs Thomas What?

Mr Smith I don't know. What was I saying?

Mrs Thomas The world.

Mr Smith It's full of people, and they're all monsters,
except you. I love them. I'll pray for them in my grave. I
used to hate them. You don't condemn me for that now
do you?

Mrs Thomas If I don't go to bed now, I know Gareth will
be upset.

Mr Smith He'll be upset will he?

Mrs Thomas We agreed I'd go up by ten o'clock.

Mr Smith Did we?

Mrs Thomas He and I.

Mr Smith He and I?

Mrs Thomas Me.

Mr Smith Me. (*Pause.*) I don't know, do you mind if I
finish what I'm saying?

Mrs Thomas No, it's alright. Go on.

Mr Smith All my life you've been a clock-watcher.

Mrs Thomas All your life?

Mr Smith All my life, you've plagued me with your condescending attitude, whenever I'm talking, you pretend to be bored.

Mrs Thomas I know. I do. I'm sorry.

Mr Smith It's not boring what I'm saying, because it's about the only good thing in any of us, and that is the ability to feel pity for us all together, forgiveness, love, tears, but my life hasn't been full of tears, in fact I don't know what the hell I've been doing. I can just vaguely remember thinking it was going to be full of poetry and then... Oh God I feel so sorry, I've not done what I should have... I'm so sorry for everyone and everything... I have not lived! A long life of poetry I thought it would be, then those twenty, thirty or forty years happened and all I did was... I don't know, to unpack or pack or something.

Mrs Thomas You have done enough in your life, don't be sad.

Mr Smith I forgot to. It slipped by. I regret, I regret! I want it back, I'm so sorry!

Mrs Thomas My darling.

She comforts him, puts her arms around his shoulders, he cries.

Pause. He looks up.

Mr Smith This isn't fear. It's something worse. It's regret, it's...

Mrs Thomas You've nothing to regret...except me of course.

Mr Smith I do regret you.

Mrs Thomas I have to go up now.

He looks at her for a long while. She stands completely still.

———

VIII

Next day. In his room. He is by his window, which is open. Outside there is wind and rain.

She comes in, sees him there, continues into the room, saying nothing. After a while he closes the window because she is there and goes to join her.

Mr Smith What are your plans for today then?

Mrs Thomas I told you, we're leaving at six this evening. Gareth is keen to get back now.

Mr Smith It's odd, because you've barely arrived.

Mrs Thomas I think he's been very patient. It's been difficult.

Mr Smith Yes, Gareth is good at waiting. It's just that I was expecting you to stay longer.

Mrs Thomas So was I, but it didn't work out that way. You have to see it from his point of view.

Mr Smith Do I? I'm glad I never said that to you about my wife.

Mrs Thomas Why glad?

Mr Smith Your likely response.

Mrs Thomas Well yes, I would have finished it.

Mr Smith There you are!

Mrs Thomas But you and I aren't together now. Why are you being like this?

Mr Smith I want to squeeze it all in before you go. It's my last chance to tell you what a – (*Stops himself.*) Is there nothing I could do or say?

Mrs Thomas No. Nothing at all.

Mr Smith That's very…unbending.

Mrs Thomas Except one thing.

Mr Smith Won't you tell me what it is?

Mrs Thomas No, I don't want to.

Mr Smith Oh. Doesn't that make it a bit difficult for me to…

Mrs Thomas Alright, alright… (*Irritably, not really listening.*)

Pause.

Mr Smith You know you're very irritable with me…

Mrs Thomas I'm sorry.

Mr Smith I don't like the way you say 'I'm sorry' either. There's something, I don't know, self-centred about it.

Mrs Thomas Self-centred?

Mr Smith Yes! But also arrogant and… Well, you *know* you're cold and insincere.

Mrs Thomas I see.

Mr Smith Yes, don't pretend to be surprised or insulted, you know yourself what you have become.

Mrs Thomas Yes. I do. Is this what you wanted to say to me before I leave?

Mr Smith I wanted to tell you – (*He is short of breath.*)

Mrs Thomas Can't you breathe?

Mr Smith I'm fine. I'm nervous. Will I get it all out in time. No, you see, it's because you've lost yourself.

Mrs Thomas Have I?

Mr Smith You were a sweet girl, you were clever, you were beautiful, passionate…and on occasion, you could even be funny, although maybe that's stretching it a bit... (*Takes a deep breath, he is struggling.*) This is chaos.

Mrs Thomas I think you should relax. We can talk later.

Mr Smith We'll talk now.

Mrs Thomas I am what you made me.

Mr Smith Well, I'm very sorry to hear that because most of the time you are a hypocrite. Sorry I said that already.

Mrs Thomas You told me all of this thirty years ago.

Mr Smith Yes I remember. I remember the, almost, pleasure I got from screaming it at you in the street. Of course, shouting at you in the street was not, as we know, something you were normally willing to tolerate, but I broke the sacred rule and told you what you were so that everyone could see it and hear it!

Mrs Thomas Yes, I remember.

Mr Smith Yes you little prig, you allowed it that time because you realised that I'd finally seen right through you.

Mrs Thomas How can you still be so angry about it after so many years?

Mr Smith Listen! Listen!

Mrs Thomas What is it?

Mr Smith The sound of your tyranny echoing down through the years! Hear it?

Mrs Thomas I don't want to go through all this now.

Mr Smith I bet you don't! You think you've got away with it.

Mrs Thomas It can't have been all that bad.

Mr Smith Bad? It was beautiful. But would I have the courage to blaspheme in order to tell the truth? Do you remember the atmosphere?

Mrs Thomas If you mean do I remember when we were falling in love, yes I do.

Mr Smith Yes call it falling in love, where I learned in the school of your refined feelings –

Mrs Thomas Please, this isn't doing either of us any good.

Mr Smith – your sense of dignity and decency, I learnt the *extreme care* to be taken to avoid hurting the one you love.

Mrs Thomas I was lovesick and lonely and you took care of me. The circumstances were all your fault after all.

Mr Smith I was glad to take care of you.

Mrs Thomas I was your responsibility!

Mr Smith Quite right. And I never said no to you once, did I.

Mrs Thomas No. You were a thousand *yes*es that meant no.

Mr Smith I jumped through every hoop you wanted me to.

Mrs Thomas You're not reproaching me for having been a sensitive young girl are you?

Mr Smith God forbid! To reproach you for anything was a sign of wickedness.

Mrs Thomas I simply didn't trust you any more if you were nasty to me. And I still don't.

Mr Smith That's a great insurance against criticism.

Mrs Thomas I taught you some standards which you lacked.

Mr Smith You mean you taught me with threats to tread as if on a fine glass dome.

Mrs Thomas You admit yourself you came from a brawling background don't you?

Mr Smith Yes, that was my excuse, what was yours?

Mrs Thomas (*Silence.*)

Mr Smith There it is again! The silence, the threat! Hear it again? Which word or which omission has injured you and made you indignant? But fortunately I learnt the map of hurt long ago – it was the finest painting of the heart drawn by the solemn hand of a young woman whose breast was pierced with a hundred invisible arrows.

Mrs Thomas It's very nice that you mock now what you once loved.

Mr Smith Oh yes, I loved you alright: the stern, pious little teacher. I began to etch the map of your heart onto my own just so that I might know it better. It's still there. (*He punches his heart.*)

Mrs Thomas Is it?

Mr Smith Yes, but you aren't likely to be able to recognize it.

Mrs Thomas Oh? And why is that?

Mr Smith Let's see shall we? Because, as soon as our positions reversed and I had lost you and was on my knees, you became the reverse image of yourself –

Mrs Thomas I see.

Mr Smith You completely changed the rules.

Mrs Thomas Shsh!! Please stop raising your voice!

Mr Smith Where in the past you expected the utmost care to be taken of your sensitive little heart – there you were most crude and heedless in how you treated mine.

Mrs Thomas (*A bit weakly.*) It was difficult for me.

Mr Smith Where you made it sacrilege for me to offer an excuse for anything, even a good one – well there you –

Mrs Thomas I only tried to explain certain circumstances.

Mr Smith – your new mouth was stuffed with banalities of the worst most hurtful kind. Now, isn't that surprising? Doesn't it make the very best seem like the very worst? Doesn't it take the ground from under your feet? Don't you find? Well?

Mrs Thomas It's not perhaps very surprising actually…

Mr Smith No! Not surprising! No, I've realised that.

Mrs Thomas Maybe it is a relief, maybe it's better, more realistic. Life has to be lived after all.

Mr Smith Yes! Yes! That's good, that's exactly the kind of thing she said!

Mrs Thomas I had already spoken love to you and it got me nowhere, so I changed.

Mr Smith Yes, now that it was someone else on the receiving end and not you, you changed everything.

Mrs Thomas You told me not to expect perfection.

Mr Smith I appealed to you in the name of what you used to be and you just said that was a phase passed. 'I was wrong to be like that,' you said.

Mrs Thomas Well, there you are then, I admitted it.

Mr Smith The one and only time you admitted to being wrong was when you knew you weren't.

Mrs Thomas You had changed me.

Mr Smith Well, you certainly were a new person, one that the old one would have despised.

Mrs Thomas Yes, I agree with you. I never thought I would have been reduced to so little.

Mr Smith To save yourself from having to feel anything you destroyed the girl I loved.

Mrs Thomas I had already felt enough by that time, I think, don't you?

Mr Smith So, you put the crowbar into yourself, and split yourself into two people, one was left in my heart and the other claimed to be you. Do you remember any of this, or has it been erased by thirty years of lying?

Mrs Thomas Oh yes, I remember it. I remember every second...

Mr Smith Well, when you cracked yourself into two you also split my own heart and cracked open my mind with it. Do you remember why?

Mrs Thomas Because I was etched there.

Mr Smith The crevice you had made, and it was the blackest emptiest abyss, worse than life and worse than nothing – I was there on the edge of that precipice, you understand what I'm saying don't you??

Mrs Thomas Yes.

There is a noise on the stairs then on the small landing outside the bedroom door.

What was that?

Mr Smith It sounds like Gareth has chosen this moment to go to the toilet.

Mrs Thomas Do you mind if we keep this quiet, at least?

Mr Smith Quiet? Certainly. So do you remember your worst crime?

Mrs Thomas I haven't committed a crime

Mr Smith We were speaking on the phone, I told you I was in trouble.

Mrs Thomas Tell me quickly, I've got to go.

Mr Smith Tell you quickly. Haven't you got time to listen?

Mrs Thomas It's late…

Mr Smith Even now.

Mrs Thomas Go on, just tell me. (*She looks at her watch.*)

Mr Smith We were on the phone…

Mrs Thomas Yes, yes.

Mr Smith …I tried not to make it too alarming, but I said, 'I am standing on the edge of the abyss holding hands with a girl who's just like you, she keeps shoving me about up here, it's getting dangerous, I think we're about to fall in…' God help me I was desperate…

Mrs Thomas Yes.

Mr Smith And what did you say?

Mrs Thomas That, I can't remember.

Mr Smith You said – nothing. There was a rustling sound, I said, 'Are you there?' You said, 'Yes. I am finishing something.' I said, 'What???' 'I'm sorry,' you said. 'I'm tidying up. I never get any time to tidy up.'

Mrs Thomas Oh.

She remembers the event and looks at him in shame and with a moment's trepidation.

Pause. He looks at her to see that she remembers.

Mr Smith And into that abyss I should have thrown the beautiful sacred, Tyrant of the Fragile Heart that you once were.

Mrs Thomas Why?

The old-fashioned toilet flushes, a door opens and closes, footsteps just outside the door.

Mr Smith To forget about her. You'd obviously finished with her. Why destroy myself by keeping faith with her, once you had abandoned her.

Mrs Thomas (*Repressing the violence of her reaction into a loud whispered shout.*) It was *you* that abandoned her! If *you* hadn't abandoned her I wouldn't have had to!!

Mr Smith I maybe abandoned her, but you tried to kill her off entirely.

Mrs Thomas I succeeded.

Mr Smith No you didn't. She still lives inside me and she's the one I *will* take to the grave with me! Not you!

Mrs Thomas No!!

She runs at him, screaming and tearing at him as if she is trying to take out the girl she had once been from inside his heart and mind, and to take her place.

No, it's not true. It's me, it's me. I *didn't* kill her, I didn't!

He throws his arms around her and holds her as tightly as he can to contain her violence and to limit the noise of her screams. Her struggle finally subsides.

You heard me offering to stay and look after you.

Mr Smith Alright, it's alright. (*He is breathless from the effort.*)

Mrs Thomas That was her wasn't it?

Mr Smith That was her, yes.

Mrs Thomas And that was me! I'm her, I'm still her, I still am. Just not always. I can't afford to be her all the time, it hurts too much, I had to find a way of living, but I am her!

Mr Smith (*Silence.*)

Mrs Thomas You don't know how lonely it was, you were never there, I was rotting with misery and I was still only a child, but with the grief of a whole lifetime eating my soul. It still does, and that's what you see now, someone who has been eaten up and left for dead. Don't you remember, you seem to have left the main facts out of your description. I was a thousand *no*s that meant yes.

Mr Smith I do remember.

Mrs Thomas Then don't ever say I'm not her, that I'm not myself, I'm not who I am, because I have paid for her in years and years of loneliness and morbidity when I was young and beautiful and should have been in the arms of love, not lying on my cold bed on my own like in a coffin.

Long pause.

We can't have this kind of scene in here. For God's sake.

Mr Smith I'm sorry. But it was you that shouted.

Mrs Thomas Let's get out of here, we'd better go for a walk or something. This is grotesque. He heard everything.

Mr Smith Alright, we'll go for a walk.

Mrs Thomas Look, I've finished with this, I don't want to carry on. Do you understand! I'm finished with this.

Mr Smith Alright then.

Mrs Thomas Just a short walk, to say goodbye.

——

IX

On the sea front. Nearly twilight. Windy.

Mrs Thomas We can't be out here long, it's too windy, it's horrible.

Mr Smith What is it I could do or say?

Mrs Thomas Ask me to marry you.

Mr Smith (*Pause. He is greatly taken aback.*) But…

Mrs Thomas What?

Mr Smith You're already married.

Mrs Thomas Yes. Well. I didn't know if you were going to ever ask me.

Mr Smith I…do you mean you…would you leave Gareth?

Mrs Thomas I don't know if I'd have to actually leave him.

Mr Smith What do you mean?

Mrs Thomas I would have to discuss it with him.

Mr Smith Discuss it? Discuss what?

Mrs Thomas He might accept it.

Mr Smith Bigamy? He'd accept bigamy?

Mrs Thomas Yours and mine wouldn't be a real marriage.

Mr Smith Thanks very much.

Mrs Thomas Well how could it be?

Mr Smith What would it be then? I don't really get it.

Mrs Thomas It wouldn't for example be a legal marriage. I wouldn't inherit any of your money.

Mr Smith It's all yours anyway.

Mrs Thomas Don't be ridiculous.

Mr Smith If you want it.

Mrs Thomas I don't want it.

Mr Smith Then I'll give it to the government.

Mrs Thomas They probably need it. I don't.

Mr Smith Gareth may want it. He has to work pretty hard.

Mrs Thomas You can't buy me from Gareth.

Mr Smith This is becoming a little silly if you ask me.

Mrs Thomas Gareth would never sell me.

Mr Smith Well no of course not. What are we talking about?

Mrs Thomas That's for you to say.

Mr Smith So you would leave Gareth?

Mrs Thomas No.

Mr Smith He would let you marry me, in some way?

Mrs Thomas Maybe. I'd have to ask him. Well, with what you are offering, it may not require all that much on his part.

Mr Smith What am I offering? I'm lost.

Mrs Thomas I think it's a bit odd that you think I should leave Gareth.

Mr Smith I didn't say that you should.

Mrs Thomas Good. I would never leave Gareth.

Mr Smith Alright, alright, you don't have to go on about it.

Mrs Thomas There is something indecent about the way you presume some automatic superiority over any other man in my life.

Mr Smith Indecent?

Mrs Thomas And of course, it has really harmed me, over the years.

Mr Smith Has it?

Mrs Thomas Yes. It says a lot about you and very little about the facts.

Mr Smith Alright then. Now about this marriage –

Mrs Thomas Yes, what about it? We can talk about it another time. It's hardly worth discussing.

Mr Smith I see.

Mrs Thomas It's a bit disingenuous of you to pretend not to know what this is about.

Mr Smith Is it? I'm sorry about that.

Mrs Thomas Okay. Fine. Shall we go back in now?

Mr Smith As you like.

Mrs Thomas I can't bear this cold.

Pause. They don't move.

Mr Smith What is it about then?

Mrs Thomas Partly, you have to realise that things do actually change. They don't just stay the same forever. I've never really understood your, I must say, somewhat peculiar, view of people and things being the same forever, just going on and on into eternity. You say it's romantic, or faithful, but I think it's rather unpleasant and abusive.

Mr Smith I see.

Mrs Thomas I don't even understand it, and I'm not sure I want to.

Mr Smith No no.

Mrs Thomas People change.

Mr Smith Yes.

Mrs Thomas You always interpret any change as a kind of betrayal. You even try to pretend that any change in me is also a betrayal of myself. There is something very nasty about that.

Mr Smith I see what you mean.

Mrs Thomas You are afraid of life yourself, and you're afraid of signs of life in others. You need people to only exist in connection to you. I think you honestly would like to believe that everyone you know – when they're not actually in front of you – goes each home to his or her coffin and crawls inside it to wait until the next time they see you.

Mr Smith What an enchanting idea. I'm not sure you're wrong about that.

Mrs Thomas But in reality people are only partly what you see, most of each of them is other things; they go off, they leave, work, fall in love, have sex, go to the toilet, make money, make friends, develop interests and even beliefs and ideas, that are totally independent of you.

Mr Smith And is that what you've been doing? All that sex and going to the toilet and beliefs and ideas? Is that what you've been up to all these years? Is that what you want to tell me?

Mrs Thomas If you really loved me you would know it. You would wish it for me, you would pray each night that my life is full and happy and independent of you and free!

Mr Smith I do, I do. I pray each night, exactly as you say.

Mrs Thomas ...and you wouldn't resent and criticise every way in which I change and develop and became a person quite different from the one you knew.

Mr Smith If you're happy with what you have become, then so am I.

Mrs Thomas There you go!

Mr Smith No. I am content if you are. And you say you are, and so I say I am too.

Mrs Thomas I don't say that I am, when did I say that?

Mr Smith Alright, I hope you are.

Mrs Thomas You hope I am?

Mr Smith Yes.

Mrs Thomas Why?

Mr Smith Why?

Mrs Thomas Why do you 'hope' that I am happy with what I have become, as you put it?

Mr Smith I...em...

Mrs Thomas You see, I may not like what I have become. What you have to accept is – that what I have become is nothing to do with you. It's not a testimony to anything to do with you. It's not a result of anything to do with you, it's not even something that can be remedied by anything to do with you. It just is that way. Many people, most people, don't like what they have become. That's life. If you do like what you have become then lucky you. But maybe that's why nobody likes you.

Mr Smith Nobody likes me?

Mrs Thomas Oh, you know what I mean, I didn't mean nobody likes you.

Mr Smith No, I don't know what you mean. Am I supposed to take it for granted? No one likes me? Since when?

Mrs Thomas You can hardly deny you've had difficulties.

Mr Smith ?

Mrs Thomas Oh look forget it. I'm sorry. But did you hear what I said or are you going to ignore it as usual?

Mr Smith No. I heard it. You said there is no such thing as love, no such thing as loss, or faithfulness, no disappointment, no hope, we are all interchangeable.

Mrs Thomas I don't remember saying any of that. But we are, aren't we? Interchangeable. Isn't that what you have taught me?

Mr Smith No. Certainly not!

Mrs Thomas Please don't deny it. Because if you do… I shall never understand why…you could have let me go. (*She is crying, she restrains it.*)

Mr Smith (*He tries to speak.*)

Mrs Thomas No don't answer. I'm afraid your answer will kill me. You've already killed me so many times, I know, but how many deaths can I be expected to die?

Pause.

Mr Smith You can't cure our disappointment by pretending not to be the same person I fell in love with.

Mrs Thomas I'm not the same person.

Mr Smith But a short while ago you screamed at me that you are!

Mrs Thomas Yes, well, it's just like with everything, like what you said. It could have been a beautiful life, but it isn't. It's the same life, but it has been violated.

Mr Smith Well…you are still in there, somewhere…

Mrs Thomas You want to comfort yourself by believing that at the end of your life, you can be reunited with the girl you sent away. But you can't; she no longer exists. You destroyed her.

Mr Smith And is that the story you have invented to comfort yourself? It's very cold comfort.

Silence.

In fact, I can't see where any comfort lies in that at all. Except in a kind of vengeful sulk. A sulk which, I must say, proves only that you haven't changed at all.

Mrs Thomas The comfort lies in not having to endure the horrible pain of being that girl who believed in love and faithfulness.

Mr Smith You think it's healthy to turn yourself into someone who doesn't believe in love?

Mrs Thomas Don't you think it's cruel of you to try to persuade me love exists, and then deny it to me?

Mr Smith I'm not denying it to you.

Mrs Thomas (*Corrects herself.*) Having denied it to me all my life.

Mr Smith I have always loved you, and I've always been faithful to my love for you.

Mrs Thomas If that's love, I'd rather believe it didn't exist.

Long pause.

Seagulls.

He looks up at them, she doesn't.

Very long pause.

Mr Smith Yes but…it's is all we've got left.

Long pause.

Mrs Thomas No. It's all you've got left. I've got my husband, my children, my career, and twenty years of life ahead of me.

Silence.

Very long pause.

She turns his chair away from the sea and wheels him away.

They are gone.

The sea gets rougher, gets very rough.

———

X

In his room.

The sea heard from a distance, very rough.

He is sitting near the fire, putting wood onto it.

Mr Smith The sea is very rough now.

She wanders into the room.

Mrs Thomas Hm.

Mr Smith Have you got your bags ready?

Mrs Thomas Yes.

Mr Smith Oh, I see you've even got your coat on.

Mrs Thomas Gareth has taken the bags downstairs.

Mr Smith Right.

Mrs Thomas So.

Mr Smith Hm. I think he may have to take them back up again.

Mrs Thomas Why?

Mr Smith Because the sea's too rough.

Mrs Thomas We'll survive.

Mr Smith Doubtless. However there is no ferry.

Mrs Thomas What?

Mr Smith I telephoned. It's cancelled. They can't even get out of the harbour.

Mrs Thomas They said that?

Mr Smith Exactly that. It's roughest just outside the harbour. Always is. It's a fact. A local one, but a fact nevertheless.

Mrs Thomas You're not making this up are you?

Mr Smith No.

Mrs Thomas Because we're leaving anyway.

Mr Smith Oh. Well, yes okay. Put another log on the fire would you, my wrist hurts.

Mrs Thomas There's smoke on the stairs you know.

Mr Smith Yes I know, the chimney's broken.

Mrs Thomas Yes I know.

Mr Smith Do you?

Mrs Thomas You told me.

Mr Smith Did I? Oh. Where are you off to then.

Mrs Thomas I don't know, we'll try the tunnel.

Mr Smith It's full. I mean, booked up.

Mrs Thomas (*Laughs.*) Sweetie. It can't be full. You're very sweet, but it can't be. (*She cries a little.*)

Pause.

Mr Smith It is. I phoned them.

Mrs Thomas Let me phone.

Mr Smith Okay. But I did. Really.

She goes out and down the stairs.

He puts more wood on the fire. It blazes very brightly. He stares into it. We can hear the sea, breakers crashing onto the sea wall, washing over onto the road.

Mr Smith (*He sings.*)

O
The big ship's sailing on the Illy Ally O
The Illy Ally O
The Illy Ally O
O the big ship's sailing on the Illy Ally O
Hi ho, the Illy Ally O
Hi ho, the Illy Ally O

Pause.

He puts even more wood onto the fire.

Pause.

O the big ship's sailing back again
Back again, back again,
O the big ship's sailing back again
Hi ho back again
Hi ho back again!

He laughs.

She comes in.

Silence.

Long pause.

Mrs Thomas Yes it seems you're right.

Mr Smith Rotten luck but there you are.

Mrs Thomas We'll drive down anyway and stay in a hotel and get the first boat in the morning.

Mr Smith Okay.

Mrs Thomas Why are you burning so much wood? It's roasting in here.

Mr Smith As you can imagine, a man in my position, I find a declining fire rather depressing.

Mrs Thomas (*Laughs.*) You'll have to start throwing the furniture on.

Mr Smith Yes. I'd like to burn the bed.

Mrs Thomas It's made of iron.

Mr Smith You wait until I get the fire going, it will be like a furnace: iron beds, brick houses, they'll go up in smoke. Phssst!

Mrs Thomas Are you practising for the fires of Hell?

Mr Smith It's funny that you should develop a sense of humour so late in my life. Just in time for my gallows.

Mrs Thomas I've had a lot of practice.

Mr Smith Yes you have.

Mrs Thomas Do you remember explaining gallows humour to me when I was nineteen?

Mr Smith Yes I do. You had a brain as flat as a board.

Mrs Thomas Yes.

Mr Smith Do you remember how you cried when I told you your expression made you look like a sodomised fish.

Mrs Thomas Yes. (*Cries.*)

They embrace.

———

The same.

Mr Smith I've missed you so much.

Mrs Thomas Yes.

Mr Smith I often can't bear it.

Mrs Thomas What do you do then. When you can't bear it?

Mr Smith I turn my face to the wall.

Long pause.

It nearly killed me. I mean it nearly sent me mad.

Mrs Thomas I know.

Mr Smith I couldn't even stand up out of my bed for three months.

Mrs Thomas Yes.

Mr Smith You did all you could to make it worse for me.

Mrs Thomas Yes.

Mr Smith I never recovered from what you did to me.

Mrs Thomas No. But.

Pause.

I never recovered from what you did to me.

Mr Smith No. I suppose not. But I meant to say that because of it, I am…like I am now.

Mrs Thomas How?

Mr Smith I have a kind of loneliness inside me that is like fear.

Mrs Thomas (*Silence.*)

Mr Smith You made me afraid to be alive.

Mrs Thomas (*Silence.*)

Mr Smith It never went.

And that's why you maybe owe it to me to help me now. Because I'm afraid of death. And I wouldn't have been if it hadn't been for you.

Mrs Thomas Well. It's the same for me. But who's going to help me? Am I supposed to help you to leave me again? And to be left to carry on living, alone, again?

Pause.

Mr Smith I don't actually need you to stay. I'd be lying if I said I did.

Mrs Thomas (*Silence.*)

Mr Smith I mean, Mrs Whatsit is a trained, you know, she's a fully trained cleaner, and then…later I can book a place in a home and my cousins will visit me. I have three surviving cousins, very sprightly they are. I shan't want for fruit and biscuits and the Radio Times.

Mrs Thomas Good.

Mr Smith I mean it's absurd to feel particularly lonely without particular people. I mean have you ever considered…why was it that God made the universe so vast with so little in it. A big empty place with only us in it. And to cap it all, it has become unfashionable to say we are unique. What a joke!!! Unique isn't the word for it! The loneliest creatures it is possible to imagine.

Mrs Thomas To say who is unique?

Mr Smith The human race. Aren't you following?

Mrs Thomas I don't know. Maybe it's not very democratic. What about the aliens?

Mr Smith There are no fucking aliens. We are the aliens. We are all alone with God in this nasty, dead universe. Do you think he lives at the other end of the universe or does he live down our end, do you think?

Mrs Thomas I don't know. I'd better be going.

Mr Smith Yes but, do you think it's a long journey? I think that Hell is the journey to Heaven, through the dead universe. Imagine! It could take billions of years to get there.

Mrs Thomas What are you talking about?

Mr Smith I mean, we presume that physical distance doesn't matter after you are dead, but what if it does, and why shouldn't it...? So, how will we find each other, you and me? Even if talking about space and time is only a sort of metaphor...how will we? How will we find each other, even amongst all the other dead souls. Have you ever wondered that?

Mrs Thomas Yes, I have.

Mr Smith I mean what if we don't end up next to each other on the shelf in the never-ending tomb? What then eh? This magic we all take for granted.

Mrs Thomas I don't know. There's nothing. There's just nothing. There isn't anything.

Mr Smith Let's hope not.

Pause.

Yes, let's hope not. But if there is something, I'll keep an eye out for you.

Mrs Thomas Please stop it now. I don't like this flippant, childish way of talking you have.

Mr Smith But I'm serious.

Mrs Thomas Were you? You know I can't tell these days with you. You have become like you were when you were a little boy.

Mr Smith Hm. Maybe. But you didn't actually know me when I was a little boy.

Mrs Thomas Oh I did, believe me, I did.

She picks up her bag. Stands by the door.

He sits staring ahead, his back to her and the door.

She puts her bag down and sits on the chair by the door. Stares at the back of his head. He can't see her.

End.

www.ingramcontent.com/pod-product-compliance
Ingram Content Group UK Ltd.
Pitfield, Milton Keynes, MK11 3LW, UK
UKHW020730020325
455688UK00017B/711

9 781840 026252